Leonardo

The biog

Introduction

Leonardo da Vinci was a Renaissance painter, sculptor, architect, inventor, military engineer and draftsman.

Endowed with a curious mind and a brilliant intellect, da Vinci studied the laws of science and nature, which greatly influenced his work.

His drawings, paintings and other works have influenced countless artists and engineers over the centuries.

"I have been impressed by the urgency of doing. It is not enough to know, you have to apply. It is not enough to want, you have to do" - Leonardo da Vinci

This is the descriptive and concise biography of Leonardo Da Vinci.

Table of Contents

Leonardo da Vinci

Leonardo da Vinci (Italian: *Leonardo di ser Piero da Vinci*, known as *Leonardo da Vinci*), born on April 15, 1452 in Vinci (Tuscany) and died on May 2, 1519 in Amboise (Touraine), was an Italian painter and man of universal mind, who was an artist, organizer of shows and festivals, scientist, engineer, inventor, anatomist, sculptor, architect, urban planner, botanist, musician, poet, philosopher and writer.

After his childhood in Vinci, Leonardo studied with the famous Florentine painter and sculptor Andrea del Verrocchio. His first important works were in the service of Duke Ludovico Sforza in Milan. He later worked in Rome, Bologna and Venice and spent the last three years of his life in France, at the invitation of King Francis I.

Leonardo da Vinci is often described as the archetype and symbol of Renaissance man, a universal genius, a humanist philosopher, observer and experimenter. However, it is above all as a painter that Leonardo da Vinci is recognized. Two of his works, *the Mona Lisa* and the *Last Supper*, are world famous, often copied and parodied, and his drawing of the *Vitruvian Man* is also used in many derivative works. Only about fifteen paintings have survived. This small number is mainly due to his constant and sometimes disastrous experimentation with new techniques. However, these few works, together with his notebooks containing more than 6,000 pages of notes, drawings, scientific papers and reflections on the nature of painting (collected in ten Codices, most of which were published in the 19th century), are a legacy for the generations of artists who followed him.

As an engineer and inventor, Leonardo developed ideas far ahead of his time, prototypes of airplanes, helicopters, submarines and even automobiles. Very few of his projects became reality or even viable during his lifetime, but some of his smaller inventions, such as a machine to measure the elastic limit of a cable, entered the world of manufacturing. As a scientist, Leonardo da Vinci devoted much of his life to the study of anatomy, civil engineering, optics and hydrodynamics, but without really sharing his knowledge.

Biography

The main period sources relating to Leonardo da Vinci are, on the one hand, the notebooks he wrote throughout his life and, on the other, three 16th century documents that mention him: *The Lives of the best painters, sculptors and architects*, written by the painter Giorgio Vasari, the *Anonimo Gaddiano*, an anonymous manuscript from the 1540s, and *the Libro dei sogni*, written in the 1560s by Giovanni Paolo Lomazzo, whose painting teacher was Leonardo's pupil. Leonardo's contemporaries, Antonio Billi, a Florentine merchant, and Paolo Giovio, an Italian physician and historian, wrote two shorter accounts.

Leonardo da Vinci's notebooks represent some 7,200 pages of notes and sketches written on paper and miraculously preserved until the 21st century. Written by Leonardo, they are filled with seemingly random notes, mathematical calculations, flying machines, theatrical props, birds, heads, angels, plants, weapons of war, fables, riddles, sketches and various reflections. His notebooks are an enormous source of information that can guide researchers toward understanding Leonardo's "feverish, creative, manic and sometimes exalted" mental functioning.

The Lives of the best painters, sculptors and architects by Giorgio Vasari (born in 1511, eight years before Leonardo's death) was published in 1550. The first work of art history, it was revised and completed in 1568 on the basis of more detailed interviews with people who had known Leonardo. But Vasari was a proud Florentine of his city, and he produced a dithyrambic portrait of

Leonardo: he was described alongside Michelangelo as one of the fathers of an artistic "renaissance" (the first written trace of this term). The book is a mixture of proven facts and hearsay, hagiographies and picturesque anecdotes, such as the one in which Leonardo's teacher throws his brush over his pupil's work in a fit of admiration.

The *Anonimo Gaddiano* (named after the family to which the author belonged) is an anonymous manuscript dating from around 1540 that also contains picturesque details about Leonardo and other Florentines. Here, too, some details are embellished, while others, more resplendent, appear to be accurate; for example, the knee-length pink tunics that Leonardo liked to wear at a time when long garments were fashionable.

Libro dei sogni is written by Giovanni Paolo Lomazzo. Lomazzo, after losing his sight, became a writer, and *Libro dei sogni is an* unpublished manuscript in which the author provides important information about Leonardo - and, very loquaciously, about his sexual orientation - based on interviews with one of his students.

Childhood

"Reputation grows like bread in the hands of a child. - Leonardo da Vinci

Leonardo da Vinci was born on the night of Friday, April 14 to Saturday, April 15, 1452, between 9:00 and 10:30 p.m. He was born in the house of a small tenant farmer in the Tuscan village of Anchiano, a hamlet near the city of

Vinci. According to tradition, he was born in the house of a small tenant in the Tuscan village of Anchiano, a hamlet near the city of Vinci, but perhaps he was born in Vinci itself. The child was the result of an illegitimate love affair between Messer Piero Fruosino di Antonio da Vinci, a 25-year-old notary and descendant of a family of notaries, and a 22-year-old woman whose first name, Caterina, is known only from documents of the time.

Ser Piero da Vinci came from a family of notaries for at least four generations; his grandfather became chancellor of the city of Florence. However, Antonio, Ser Piero's father and Leonardo's grandfather, married the daughter of a notary and preferred to retire to Vinci and lead a quiet life as a country gentleman, taking advantage of the income from the estates he owned in the city. Although in some documents he is named with the particle *Ser*, in official documents he is not entitled to this title: everything seems to show that he has no title and that he never even exercised a definite profession. Ser Piero, son of Antonio and father of Leonardo, picked up the torch of his ancestors and succeeded in Pistoia and then in Pisa, before settling in Florence around 1451. His office was located in the Palazzo del Podestà, the magistrates' building opposite the Palazzo Vecchio, the seat of government, then called Palazzo della Signoria. Monasteries, religious orders, the city's Jewish community and even the Medici called on his services.

Although the biographer Anonimo Gaddiano describes her as a "daughter of a good family", it is traditionally said that Leonardo's mother, Caterina, was the daughter of poor peasants and, therefore, far removed from Ser Piero's social class. According to the controversial conclusions of a 2006 fingerprint study, she could be a Middle Eastern slave. However, since 2017, research carried out on communal and parish documents or tax records tend to identify her with Caterina di Meo Lippi, daughter of small farmers, born in 1436 and orphaned at the age of 14.

Leonardo seems to have been baptized on the Sunday following his birth. The ceremony took place in the church of Vinci by the parish priest in the presence of the notables of the town and important aristocrats of the area. Ten godparents - an exceptional number - witnessed the baptism: all lived in the town of Vinci and among them was Piero di Malvolto, Ser Piero's godfather and owner of Leonardo's native farm. The day after the baptism, Ser Piero returned to his business in Florence. Thus, he arranged for Caterina to quickly marry a local farmer and coppersmith friend of da Vinci's family, Antonio di Piero del Vaccha, known as "Accattabriga (quarrelsome)": perhaps he did this to avoid gossip over the abandonment of a mother and child. It seems that the child remained with his mother during the time of his weaning - about 18 months - and then was entrusted to his paternal grandfather, with whom he spent the next four years, accompanied by his uncle Francesco. The maternal and paternal families continued to maintain good relations: Accattabriga worked in a kiln rented by being Piero and they regularly appeared as witnesses in contracts and notarial acts for each other. In fact, the childhood memories narrated by the adult Leonardo allow us to understand that he considers himself a child of love. He wrote: "If coitus is performed with great love and great mutual desire, the child will be of great intelligence and full of spirit, vivacity and grace.

At the age of five, in 1457, Leonardo went to his father's house in Vinci. It was an important house with a small garden in the heart of the city, right next to the castle walls. Ser Piero married the sixteen-year-old daughter of a wealthy Florentine shoemaker, Albiera degli Amadori, but she died in childbirth in 1464. Ser Piero married four more times. From the last two marriages his ten brothers and two legitimate sisters were born. Leonardo seems to have good relations with his successive mothers-in-law: thus Albiera has a particular affection for the child. In a note, he also describes his father's last wife, Lucrezia Guglielmo Cortigiani, as a "dear and gentle mother".

Leonardo was not educated by his parents: his father lived mainly in Florence and his mother took care of the other five children he had after his marriage. Therefore, it was his uncle Francesco, 15 years his senior, and his paternal grandparents who provided him with an education. His grandfather Antonio passed on to him a taste for observing nature, constantly telling him "Po l'occhio! ("Open your eyes!")". His grandmother Lucia di ser Piero di Zoso was also very close to him: a ceramist, she was perhaps the person who introduced him to the arts.

Although he considered him his own son from birth, Ser Piero did not legitimize Leonardo, who therefore could not become a notary. Moreover, belonging to an intermediate social category between *the dotti* and *the non-dotti*, he could not attend one of the Latin schools where classical literature and humanities were taught and which were reserved for future members of the liberal professions and merchants from good families in the early Renaissance. As a young man, therefore, he received a rather free education with the other villagers of his age.

At the age of ten, in 1462, he entered a *scuola d'abaco* (arithmetic school) for the children of merchants and artisans where he learned the rudiments of reading, writing and, above all, arithmetic. The normal course of study was two years, and Leonardo left school around 1464, the year he was twelve years old, at which age he was sent as an apprentice to the workshop of Andrea del Verrocchio. His spelling, described by the historian of science Giorgio de Santillana as "pure chaos", is evidence of his shortcomings. Nor did he study Greek or Latin, which, as the exclusive means of science, were essential for the acquisition of scientific theory: he only learned them - and even then, imperfectly - on his own, and only at the age of 40. For Leonardo, above all a freethinker and opponent of traditional thought, this lack of training would remain a delicate matter: in the face of attacks from the intellectual world, he would willingly present himself

11

as a "man without letters" and a disciple of experience and experimentation.

Training in Verrocchio's workshop

"Learning is the only thing that the mind never exhausts, never fears and never regrets." - Leonardo da Vinci

Around 1464 - 1465 at the latest - when he was about twelve years old, Leonardo began an apprenticeship in Florence. It is not known what precipitated this decision: perhaps the death of his grandfather, or the marriage of his uncle Francesco, or even his father's second marriage. His father sensed that he had a great aptitude for painting and entrusted him to the workshop of Andrea del Verrocchio. In fact, Piero da Vinci and the Maestro were already close: several deeds relating to at least four legal agreements and rental documents for the benefit of Verocchio were passed by Leonardo's father, and the two men had their places of work not far from each other. In his biography of Leonardo, Giorgio Vasari writes: "Piero took some of his drawings and brought them to Andrea del Verrocchio, who was a good friend, and asked him if the boy could do with studying drawing." However, it seems that Verrocchio accepted the boy as an apprentice because of his talent and not because of the friendship between the two men: according to Vasari, Verrocchio was "astonished" by Leonardo's talent.

Verrocchio was a renowned artist and polymath, trained as a goldsmith and blacksmith, painter, sculptor and caster. Like most Italian artists of his time and at the time Leonardo was apprenticed there, the workshop took on various commissions, mostly for the wealthy patron Lorenzo de' Medici: mainly paintings and bronze sculptures such as that of Christ or St. Thomas, but also an elaborate tomb, festive decorations in taffeta decorated with gold and silver flowers, and the conservation of ancient works for the Medici or wealthy merchants. Mathematics, anatomy, antiquities, music and philosophy were discussed. An inventory of the study shows several tables and beds for living, a globe, books in Italian, including translations of classical poems by Petrarch and Ovid and humorous literature by Franco Sacchetti.

The Verrocchio workshop, far from being a refined art studio, is rather a store where a large number of art objects are sold and manufactured. On the first floor there is a store and its workshops, while on the upper floor craftsmen and apprentices work and live together. Verrocchio seems to have been a good and humane master, who ran his workshop collegially to the extent that many of his pupils, such as Leonardo and Botticelli, stayed with him for some years after their apprenticeship. The sculptures and paintings are mostly unsigned and are the result of collective work. The aim of the workshop is to produce works for sale rather than to promote the talent of one artist or another. In this workshop of teachers and pupils - called *bottega* in Italian - Leonardo rubbed shoulders with other peers who would become famous, such as Lorenzo di Credi, Sandro Botticelli, Perugino and Domenico Ghirlandaio.

Leonardo thus began a multidisciplinary training: he brought together the study of surface anatomy, mechanics, drawing techniques and the study of the effects of light and shadow on materials such as curtains.

13

To reproduce the effects of volume through light and shadow, Leonardo, while learning to make colors, experimented with mixing paint with transparent liquids to obtain translucent pigments. This allowed him to study the gradations of draperies, faces, trees and landscapes. This led him to develop the technique *of chiaroscuro*, which consists of using contrasts of light and shadow to create the illusion of relief and volume in two-dimensional drawings and paintings. Leonardo also studied perspective in its geometric aspect, with the help of the writings of Leon Battista Alberti, and in its luminous aspect in which objects tend to fade as they move away. This fading he represented with his technique *of sfumato, which* gave the subject vague outlines with the help of a glaze or a smooth, transparent texture.

He also took up engraving and fresco painting. It is likely that Verrochio later asked his pupil to complete his paintings, in particular the painting Tobias and the angel, where he drew the tent held by the angel and the dog walking behind the figure on the left. Verrochio, more versed in the art of sculpture, is known for his depictions of animals, generally considered "unimportant" and "weak". It is not surprising that the master entrusted the creation of the animals to his pupil Leonardo, whose keen sense of observation of nature is evident.

In 1470, in *The Baptism of Christ,* Leonardo painted the angel on the far left and partially other elements of the painting. X-ray analysis shows that much of the decoration, the body of Christ and the angel on the left are made of several layers of oil paint with very diluted pigments. According to Vasari, Leonardo so impressed Verrocchio that he decided "never to touch a brush again". In fact, after this work, Verrocchio never finished another painting alone.

But the training he received during his apprenticeship in Verrocchio's workshop seems even more extensive. Leonardo acquired knowledge of algorithmic calculus and was instructed by the prominent Florentine physician and geographer Paolo Toscanelli del Pazzo and by Benedetto dell'abbaco, who taught arithmetic in Florence.

In 1472, he finished his apprenticeship and became a master at the age of twenty. On this occasion, his name appears alongside those of Perugino and Botticelli in the *Red Book of Debtors and Creditors of the Company of St. Luke, that is,* in the register of the painters' guild of Florence, a sub-guild of the guild of physicians There are some traces of this period in Leonardo's life, such as the date of one of his earliest works, a pen and ink drawing, *Landscape of the Arno Valley (*1473). One of the first works is *The Annunciation (*1472-1475) in which he already shows his interest in *sfumato* (fog printing).

While still working in Verrocchio's workshop, Leonardo also produced in the 1470s four paintings that are mainly attributed to him: an Annunciation, two Virgins with Child and the avant-garde portrait of a Florentine woman, Ginevra de'Benci. Leonardo seems to have increasingly mastered oil painting by applying heavily diluted pigments, the Annunciation shows numerous errors of perspective and light, which nevertheless seem to testify to some of the experiments he carried out in his research on perspective.

He is still mentioned living with Verrocchio in 1476. Leonardo established himself almost immediately as an engineer: in 1478, he offered to erect the octagonal church of San Giovanni in Florence, the present baptistery, without ruining it, to add a base.

Court records from 1476 show that, along with three other men, he was accused of sodomy at Jacopo Saltarelli, a practice that was illegal in Florence at the time. All were acquitted of the charges, probably thanks to the intervention of Lorenzo de' Medici, but Leonardo had to spend two months in prison during the judicial investigation. In these same years he painted the famous series of draped studies-some of which are still discussed along with the design of the Orsanmichele (*Christ and St. Thomas*) and the Annunciation in bronze, from models made from cloth soaked in clay to allow modeling.

16

It is not known when he definitively left his master, but his first commission (an altar painting for the chapel of the Priors in the Palace of the Lordship, of which no trace of realization seems to have been preserved) was in 1478. It is possible that he remained with him for a long time simply for material reasons.

The Milan years (1482-1499)

"The painter has the Universe in his mind and in his hands. - Leonardo da Vinci

In 1482, Leonardo da Vinci was in his thirties. He left Lorenzo the Magnificent and Florence to join the court of Milan. He remained there for 17 years. The reasons for his departure are unknown and art historians are reduced to speculation. He probably found the environment surrounding Ludovico Sforza more conducive to artistic creation, as he wanted to turn the city he had just taken over into the "Athens of Italy". Perhaps he was also bitter about not having been selected for the team of Florentine painters charged with creating the decorations for the Sistine Chapel. Moreover, Vasari and the author of the *Anonimo Gaddiano state* that Lorenzo the Magnificent commissioned the painter to give his correspondent a silver lyre in the shape of a horse's skull, which Leonardo played perfectly. Finally, Leonardo arrived with the promise to deploy his engineering talents, as evidenced by a letter he had written to his host in which he described various inventions in the military field and, incidentally, the possibility of creating architectural, sculptural or painted works.

However, it was rather his quality as an artist that was first recognized, as he was then qualified at court with the title of "Florentine Apelle", in reference to the famous Greek painter of Antiquity, which gave him the hope of finding a position and, therefore, of receiving a salary rather than simply being paid for his work. Despite this recognition, commissions did not come because he was not sufficiently established in Milan and did not yet have the necessary connections.

He then benefited from a meeting with a local painter, Giovanni Ambrogio de Predis, who was well introduced at court and who made him known to the Milanese aristocracy. Leonardo was lodged by de Predis in the latter's studio and then in the house he shared with his brother Evangelista, whose address was "Parish of San Vincenzo in Pratot *intus*". The relationship was fruitful, for in April 1483 he was commissioned, together with the Predis brothers, to paint a picture for a local confraternity: the *Madonna of the Rocks*, destined to decorate an altarpiece for a newly built chapel in the church of San Francesco Maggiore. In recognition of his status, he was the only one of the three artists to bear the title "master" on the contract. It was during this period that he painted, among others, the portrait of Cecilia Gallerani, known as *The Lady with the Ermine*, a *Portrait of a Milanese Lady* (known as *La Belle Ferronnière*), a *Woman in Profile* (most likely with Ambrogio de Predis) and possibly the *Madonna Litta*. Shortly after his arrival in Milan, he

18

established his own *bottega with* collaborators such as Ambrogio de Predis and Giovanni Antonio Boltraffio, and pupils such as Marco d'Oggiono, Francesco Napoletano and, later, Salai.

Art historians are completely unaware of the course of events in Leonardo's life in the 1480s, leading some researchers to consider him isolated and reclusive. If he had known this situation, Serge Bramly believes, he would have left: on the contrary, Leonardo must have seen his position improve, albeit slowly but steadily.

He became the "organizer of the festivals and shows" given in the palace and invented successful theatrical machines. The pinnacle of his achievements in 1496 was "a masterpiece of theatrical machinery [created] for Baldassare Taccone's *Danae* in the palace of Giovan Francesco Sanseverino, where the leading actress is transformed into a star." But, in general, if his activity as an engineer was not ignored, he had to work hard to have it recognized. The episode of the plague in Milan in 1484-1485 gave him the opportunity to propose solutions to the issue of the "new city" that was then emerging. In 1487 a competition was held for the construction of the lantern tower of the Milan cathedral, in which Leonardo participated. He submitted a model during 1488-1489. Although his project was not selected, it seems that some of his ideas were taken up by the winner of the competition, Francesco di Giorgio. So much so that in the 1490s he became, along with Bramante and Gian Giacomo Dolcebuono, a leading urban and architectural engineer. In fact, the Lombard archives readily refer to him as "ingeniarius ducalis" and it was in this capacity that he was sent to Pavia.

During this time, Leonardo devoted himself to technical-scientific studies, whether of anatomy, mechanics (clocks and looms) or mathematics (arithmetic and geometry), which he scrupulously wrote down in his notebooks, probably in order to elaborate systematic treatises. For all these reasons, and although he defines himself as a "man of no letters", his writings express his anger and incomprehension at the contempt with which he felt treated by doctors due to his lack of university training.

From 1489 to 1494 he also worked on the creation of an imposing equestrian statue in honor of Francesco Sforza, Ludovico's father and predecessor. At first he planned to make a moving horse, but was forced to give up in the face of difficulties and return to a more classical solution, like that of Verrocchio. On April 20, 1493 only a large clay model was made. But the 60 tons of bronze needed for the statue were used to cast cannons for the defense of the city against the invasion of the French King Charles VIII.

On July 22, 1490, the painter noted in a notebook dedicated to the study of light, which served as a logbook, that he had welcomed a ten-year-old boy, Gian Giacomo Caprotti, into his studio in exchange for some florins given to his father. The boy quickly accumulated misdeeds. Leonardo wrote about him: "Thief, liar, stubborn, glutton"; from then on the boy earned the nickname *Salai, a* contraction of the Italian *Sala[d]ino* meaning "little devil". However, the teacher could not imagine parting with him and was very fond of him. Historians have wondered about the exact relationship between the forty-year-old and this boy, then a teenager with such a perfect face, and many see it as a confirmation of his homosexuality or, at the very least, of his taste for bad boys. Despite his poor artistic qualities, Salai integrates himself into the painter's studio.

In 1493, Leonardo was fifty years old. In his tax documents, he notes that he has a woman named Caterina in his house. He confirms it in a notebook: "On July 16/Caterina arrived on July 16, 1493". Historians do not agree on the identity of this woman: was she the painter's mother, who was then 70 years old, or a simple servant? There is nothing to confirm or disprove this hypothesis. Be that as it may, in 1490, the date of her last official record, she was certainly a widow and seems to have had no further relations with her two surviving daughters and her legitimate son. This same Caterina died in 1495 or 1496: Leonardo lists in detail the expenses of her funeral, expenses too excessive to suggest that she was a simple servant, and a new one at that.

Fact: Leonardo's major project was destroyed; the proposed statue of the Duke's father, Francesco Sforza, on horseback was to be over 25 feet tall and intended to be the largest equestrian statue in the world. Leonardo spent nearly 17 years planning the statue. But before it was finished, French forces invaded Milan in 1499.The clay sculpture was used as target practice by the victorious French soldiers, smashing it to pieces.

Artist and engineer (1503-1516)

"The human foot is a masterpiece of engineering and a work of art. - Leonardo da Vinci

In 1502, he met Niccolo Machiavelli, a Florentine "spy" in Borgia's service, and the two worked on a project to divert the *Arno* River.

On October 18, 1503, he returned to Florence, where he worked as a war engineer (he designed arquebuses, a breech-loading bombard and siege machines such as the catapult, mortar and ballista). He was also an architect and hydraulic engineer. He rejoined the guild of St. Luke and spent the years 1503 to 1505 preparing the creation of *The Battle of Anghiari*, an imposing fresco mural, with Michelangelo doing *The Battle of Cascina* on the opposite wall. He would only paint the central group of the work, the fight for the standard. Michelangelo's painting is known from a copy by Aristotle da Sangallo of 1542 and Leonardo's is known only from preparatory sketches and several copies of the central part, the best known of which is probably that of Peter Paul Rubens. Here too, Leonardo experimented with a new type of painting, inspired by Roman encaustic. He managed to master the technique on a painting of a Slav, but could not do it on the wall. The fire needed for drying was not strong enough, so the paint began to drip and was probably covered by a fresco by Giorgio Vasari. The testimonies of the time are still quite difficult to interpret today, as they contradict each other as to the size and even the execution of the painting.

Leonardo was consulted on several occasions as an expert, in particular to study the stability of the bell tower of the basilica of San Miniato al Monte and during the choice of the site for Michelangelo's *David*, where his opinion was opposed to that of his rival. It was during this period that he presented to the city of Florence his project for the detour of the Arno River, which aimed to create a waterway capable of linking Florence to the sea and controlling the terrible floods. This period was important for the scientific training of Leonardo, who experimented in his hydraulic research. In 1504, he returned to work in Milan, which was now under the control of Maximilian Sforza, thanks to the support of Swiss mercenaries. Many of the most prominent students and followers of painting met or worked with Leonardo in Milan, such as Bernardino Luini, Giovanni Antonio Boltraffio and Marco d'Oggiono.

His father died on July 9, 1504 and Leonardo was excluded from the inheritance because of his illegitimacy; however, his uncle later made him his sole heir. That same year, Leonardo undertook anatomical studies and attempted to classify his innumerable sketches. He began work on *the Mona Lisa* (1503-1506 and 1510-1515), which is usually considered a portrait of the Mona Lisa del Giocondo, born Lisa Maria Gherardini. However, many interpretations of this painting are still debated.

In 1505, he studied the flight of birds and wrote the *Codex of Turin,* also known as the *Codex on the Flight of Birds.* From then on, observations, experiments and *a posteriori* reconstructions followed. A year later, the government of Florence allowed him to join the French governor of Milan, Charles d'Amboise, who kept him with him, despite the lordship's protests. Leonardo is torn between the French and the Tuscans; the court urges him to finish *The Virgin of the Rocks* with his pupil Giovanni Ambrogio de Predis, while he works on *The Battle of Anghiari.*

The painter became the sole heir of his uncle Francesco in 1507, but Leonardo's brothers initiated a process to annul the will. Leonardo turned to Charles d'Amboise and Florimond Robertet to intervene on his behalf. Louis XII of France was in Milan and Leonardo was once again the organizer of the festivities in the Lombard capital.

In 1508, he lived in the house of Piero di Braccio Martelli with the sculptor Giovanni Francesco Rustici in Florence, but went to live in Milan, at the *Porta Orientale of* the parish of Santa Babila. Louis XII soon returned to Italy and entered Milan in May 1509. Almost immediately, he led his armies against Venice, and Leonardo followed the king as military engineer; he was present at the battle of Agnadel. Upon the death of governor Charles d'Amboise in 1511 and after the battle of Ravenna in 1512, France abandoned Milan. This second period in Milan allowed Leonardo da Vinci to deepen his research in pure science. The publication in 1509 of Giorgio Valla's *De expendentis et fugiendis rebus* undoubtedly had a great influence on him.

In September 1513, Leonardo da Vinci left for Rome to work for Giuliano de' Medici, brother of Pope Leo X and member of the wealthy and powerful family of the same name. Both Raphael and Michelangelo were very active in the Vatican at this time. In contrast to the success of the Sangallos, Leonardo was entrusted with only modest missions and does not seem to have participated either in the construction of the numerous Roman fortresses that would mark the evolution of poliorcetica, or in the beautification of the capital. Worse still, his painting in itself no longer seems to be relevant and he took refuge in another specialty, perhaps his favorite, hydraulics, with a project for the draining of the Pontine marshes, belonging to Duke Julien de Medici. In 1514, the painter created the series "Floods", which is a partial response to the version offered by Michelangelo in the Sistine Chapel.

"The Medici *created me, the Medici destroyed me*," wrote Leonardo da Vinci, no doubt to underscore the disappointments of his stay in Rome. He probably thought he would never be allowed to prove himself in a major project. No doubt potential patrons were put off by his instability, his quick discouragement, and his difficulty in completing what he undertook.

From September 1513 to 1516, Leonardo spent much of his time living in the Belvedere courtyard of the Palazzo Apostolico, where both Michelangelo and Raphael were active. He received an allowance of 33 ducats a month and, according to Vasari, decorated a lizard with scales dipped in mercury. The pope commissioned a painting on an unknown subject, but cancelled it when he learned that the artist was developing a new type of varnish. He fell ill in what was perhaps the first of the attacks that led to his death.

Last years in France (1516-1519)

"For once you have tasted flight, you will walk the earth with your eyes fixed on the sky, for there you have been and there you will long to return." - Leonardo da Vinci

In September 1515, the new king of France, Francis I, reconquers Milan in the battle of Marignano. In November 1515, Leonardo works on a new project for the Medici quarter in Florence. On December 19, he is present in Bologna for the meeting between Francis I and

Pope Leo X. Francis I commissions Leonardo to design a mechanical lion that can walk and whose chest opens to reveal lilies. It is not known for what occasion this lion was designed, but it may be related to the king's arrival in Lyon or to the peace talks between the king and the pope.

In 1516 he went to work in France with his assistant painter Francesco Melzi y Salai, where his new patron and protector, King Francis I, installed him in the mansion of Cloux, now the Clos Lucé castle, owned by his mother Louise of Savoy.

At the age of 64, Leonardo da Vinci arrives in France, bringing with him three of his major paintings: *St. John the Baptist*, *St. Anne, The Virgin and Child Jesus Playing with a Lamb*, and *La Gioconda*. According to legend, he made this journey across the Alps on a mule, but there is no document of the time to prove it. He could have arrived by boat and then taken horses.

At the Château du Clos Lucé, Leonardo was thus close to the Château d'Amboise, the king's residence. The king appointed him "first painter, first engineer and first architect of the king" with an annual pension of one thousand ecus. Perhaps the French court was more interested in the painter and the artist than in the engineer, and until then, only the French had been attached to the illustrious Florentine as an artist: in Italy, he had only been employed as an engineer.

In giving him the Château du Clos Lucé, Francis I told Leonardo: "Here Leonardo, you will be free to dream, to think and to work". He was not the first artist to receive this honor; Andrea Solario and Giovanni Giocondo had preceded him a few years earlier.

At Le Clos Lucé, Leonardo worked as an engineer, architect and director, organizing sumptuous receptions and parties for the Court. He inspired the thinking and fashion around him. He worked on numerous projects for the king.

Francis I was fascinated by Leonardo da Vinci and considered him as a father. According to legend, the Château du Clos Lucé and the Château d'Amboise were linked by a subway passage that allowed the sovereign to visit the man of science in total discretion.

He designed and built a new residence in Romorantin for Queen Louise of Savoy (mother of Francis I), based on a pre-existing medieval castle, incorporating a river diversion on the Sauldre. The diversion, urbanization and earthworks took place between 1516 and 1518. Construction began, a 70-meter long wing was built, but the work was left unfinished in 1519, perhaps because of the plague, but more likely because of Leonardo's death. The wing built by Louise of Savoy was destroyed in 1723. In addition to Leonardo's plans in the *Codex Atlanticus*, many archaeological remains remain today, such as the ruins of the castle and the embankments, which make this unfinished project a prototype of the castle of Chambord and its famous spiral staircase, whose architect Domenico di Cortona came to meet Leonardo in 1518 at Clos Lucé.

He outlined a project for a canal between the Loire and the Saône and organized festivities, such as the one the king gave at the Château d'Argentan in October 1517 in honor of his sister Marguerite d'Angoulême.

A paralysis affected Leonardo da Vinci at the end of his life. Antonio de Beatis, secretary to Cardinal Louis of Aragon, when the two visited Leonardo da Vinci in Amboise in 1517, explained how the master had difficulties and how the students helped him.

"Although from him, having come to him a certain paralysis on the right, you can no longer expect anything good. He trained a Milanese designer who works very well. And although Leonardo da Vinci cannot color with that usual smoothness, he can also make drawings and teach others."

On April 23, 1519, Leonardo da Vinci, who had been ill for several months, drew up his will before a notary in Amboise. The letter of naturalization granted by Francis I allowed him to circumvent the law of negotiation. He asked that a priest receive him in confession and give him the last rites. He died of illness on May 2, 1519 in the castle of Clos Lucé, at the age of 67.

"While I thought I was learning to live, I have been learning to die." - Leonardo da Vinci

The tradition that he died in the arms of Francis I is told by Giorgio Vasari in the *Lives of the best painters, sculptors and architects*. It is possible that it is based on an erroneously literal interpretation of an epitaph, collected by Vasari in the 1550 edition of the *Lives*, but which no longer appears in the 1568 edition. This inscription - which has never been seen on any monument - contains the words "Sinu Regio", which can mean literally: *in the bosom of a king*; but also metaphorically: *in the affections of a king,* and may be an allusion to Leonardo's death in a royal castle. Moreover, at that time the Court was at the castle of Saint-Germain-en-Laye, where the queen was giving birth to the future Henry II on March 31 - and the royal orders issued on [May 1] are dated there. The diary of François I does not mention any trip of the king until July. Finally, Leonardo's pupil Francesco Melzi, to whom he bequeathed his books and brushes and who was the custodian of his will, wrote a letter to the great painter's brother recounting the death of his master. Not a word is said about the aforementioned circumstance which, had it been true, would surely not have been forgotten.

According to his last will, sixty beggars followed his procession to the collegiate church of Saint-Florentin, in the castle of Amboise, where he was buried. The bones attributed to Leonardo da Vinci are believed to be placed since 1874 under the tombstone of the chapel of Saint-Hubert, within the walls of the castle of Amboise and overlooking the city. His tomb was reconstructed between 1934 and 1936 by the sculptor Francis La Monaca.

Leonardo da Vinci, who was a bachelor all his life and never had a wife or children, bequeathed his considerable oeuvre to his favorite disciple and pupil from the age of ten, Francesco Melzi, for publication. In particular, he gave him his manuscripts, notebooks, documents and instruments.

After accompanying him to France, he remained close to Leonardo da Vinci until his death. However, he did not publish any of Leonardo's works and many of the paintings - including the *Mona Lisa* - that he still had in his workshop, some of which had already been sold to François I, were bequeathed to Salai during his stay at Clos Lucé in 1518. Leonardo's vineyards were divided between Salai, another pupil and disciple highly esteemed by Leonardo and who entered his service at the age of 15, and his servant Battista de Vilanis. The lands were bequeathed to Leonardo's brothers and his servant Mathurine received a black coat with fur trimmings.

Twenty years after Leonardo's death, Francis I told the sculptor Benvenuto Cellini:

"There was no other man born in the world who knew as much as Leonardo, not so much in painting, sculpture and architecture, but he was a great philosopher."

Relationships and influences

Leonardo in Florence: masters and contemporaries

Leonardo began his apprenticeship with Andrea del Verrocchio in 1466, the year Verrocchio's teacher, the great sculptor Donatello, died. The painter Paolo Uccello, whose early experiments with perspective influenced the development of landscape painting, was already very old. The painters Piero della Francesca and Fra Filippo Lippi, the sculptor Luca della Robbia and the architect and writer Leon Battista Alberti were also in their 60s. The most renowned artists of the next generation are Leonardo's teachers: Andrea del Verrocchio, Antonio Pollaiuolo and the sculptor Mino da Fiesole.

Leonardo's youth was spent in a house in Florence adorned with the works of these artists and of Donatello's contemporaries, Masaccio - whose figurative and realistic frescoes are imbued with emotion - and Lorenzo Ghiberti, whose *Paradise Gate* shows the complexity of his compositions, combining architectural work and attention to detail. Piero della Francesca made a detailed study of perspective and was the first painter to make a scientific study of light. These studies and the treatises of Leone Battista Alberti must have had a profound effect on young artists and, in particular, on Leonardo's own observations and works of art.

Masaccio's depiction of Adam and Eve naked emerging from paradise, with Adam without his genitals - masked by a fig leaf - creates a very expressive image of the human form that would greatly influence painting, especially as they are expressed in three dimensions through an innovative use of light and shadow that Leonardo would develop in his own work. Renaissance humanism, which influenced Donatello's *David*, can be seen in Leonardo's later paintings, especially *St. John the Baptist*.

Florence was then ruled by Lorenzo de' Medici and his younger brother Julian, who was killed in the Pazzi conspiracy in 1478. Ludovico Sforza, who ruled Milan between 1479 and 1499 and to whom Leonardo was sent as ambassador to the Medici court, was also his contemporary.

Also through the Medici, Leonardo met ancient humanist philosophers, such as Marsilio Ficino, a proponent of Neoplatonism, and Cristoforo Landino, author of commentaries on classical writings. Giovanni Pico della Mirandola was also associated with the Academy of Physicians. Leonardo later wrote in the margin of a diary, "The Medici made me and the Medici destroyed me"; but the meaning of this comment remains disputed.

Although the three "giants" of the High Renaissance are mentioned together, Leonardo da Vinci, Michelangelo and Raphael are not of the same generation. Leonardo was 23 when Michelangelo was born and 31 when Raphael was born. Raphael died in 1520, a year after da Vinci, and Michelangelo lived another forty-five years.

Assistants and students

"All knowledge that ends in words will die as quickly as it was born, with the exception of the written word: that is its mechanical part." - Leonardo da Vinci

Gian Giacomo Caprotti da Oreno, known as "*il Salaino*" ("*the* little devil") or Salai, was described by Giorgio Vasari as "a graceful and handsome young man, with fine curly hair, in whom Leonardo was enchanted". Salai entered Leonardo's service in 1490 at the age of 10. Their relationship was not an easy one. A year later, Leonardo listed the boy's faults as "thief," "liar," "stubborn," and "glutton." The "imp" had stolen money and valuables on at least five occasions, and had spent a fortune on clothes, including twenty-four pairs of shoes. However, Leonardo's notebooks from the early years of their relationship contain many images of the teenager. Salai remained his servant and assistant for the next thirty years.

In 1506, Leonardo took 15-year-old Francesco Melzi, the son of a Lombard aristocrat, as a pupil. Melzi became Leonardo's life companion and was considered his favorite pupil. He went to France with Leonardo and Salai, and stayed with him until his death. Salai left France in 1518 to return to Milan. There he built a house in the vineyard of Leonardo's estate, which he eventually inherited. In 1525, Salai died a violent death, either murdered or as a result of a duel.

Salai executed several paintings under the name "Andrea Salai", but, although Giorgio Vasari states that Leonardo "taught him much about painting", his work is generally considered to be of lesser artistic value than that of other pupils of Leonardo, such as Marco d'Oggiono or Giovanni Antonio Boltraffio. In 1515, he painted a nude version of *the Mona Lisa*, known as "Monna Vanna". At his death in 1525, the *Mona Lisa* belonging to Salai was valued at five hundred and five lire, an exceptionally high value for a small portrait.

Giovanni Antonio Boltraffio and Marco d'Oggiono joined Leonardo's workshop when he returned to Milan, but many other lesser-known pupils were also present, such as Giovanni Ambrogio de Predis, Bernardino de Conti, Francesco Napoletano and Andrea Solario.

Privacy

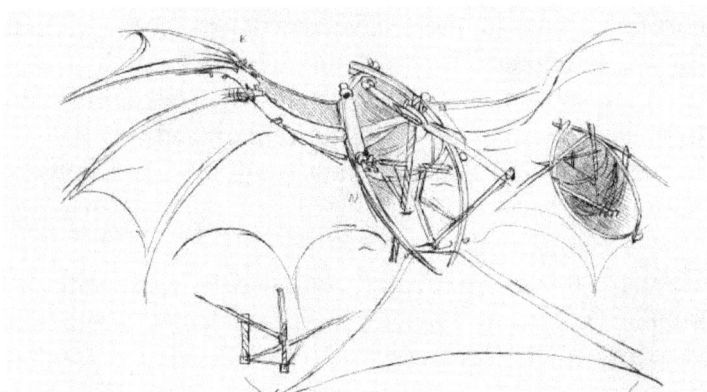

Leonardo da Vinci had many friends who were renowned in their respective fields or who have had an important influence on history. Among them were the mathematician Luca Pacioli, with whom he collaborated on a book, Cesare Borgia, in whose service he spent two years, Lorenzo de' Medici and the physician Marcantonio della Torre. He met Michelangelo, whose rival he had been, and maintained an "intimate connivance" with Niccolo Machiavelli, the two having developed a close epistolary friendship. Among his friends were also Franchini Gaffurio and Isabella d'Este. Leonardo does not seem to have had close relationships with women, except with Isabella. During a trip to Mantua he painted a portrait of her, which seems to have been used to create a painting, now lost. He was also a friend of the architect Jacopo Andrea da Ferrara until his murder.

Beyond friendship, Leonardo kept his private life a secret. During his lifetime, his extraordinary gifts of invention, his "exceptional physical beauty", his "infinite grace", his "great strength and generosity" and the "formidable breadth of his mind", as described by Vasari, aroused curiosity. Many authors have speculated on the various aspects of Leonardo's personality. His sexuality has often been the subject of study, analysis and speculation. This trend began in the mid-sixteenth century and was revived in the nineteenth and twentieth centuries, especially by Sigmund Freud.

Leonardo's most intimate relationships were with his pupils: Salai and Francesco Melzi. Melzi wrote that Leonardo's feelings were a mixture of love and passion. Since the 16th century these relationships have been described as erotic in nature. Since then authors have written extensively about his homosexuality, including his alleged pederasty, and the role of this sexuality in his art, particularly in the androgynous and erotic impression manifested in *Bacchus* and more explicitly in several of his drawings. However, the artist's supposedly platonic and courtly, even repressed, homosexuality remains highly hypothetical, and it is difficult to comment on Leonardo's morality.

Leonard is so passionate about nature and animals that he buys caged birds to set them free. He was also a very good musician. It is believed that Leonardo was left-handed and ambidextrous, which would explain his use of specular writing.

Paints

Despite the relatively recent knowledge and admiration of Leonardo as a scientist and inventor, his immense fame for most of the last four hundred years has rested on his achievements as a painter and a handful of works-authenticated or attributed to him-that have been considered among the finest masterpieces ever created.

These paintings are famous for many reasons and qualities that have been much imitated by students and widely discussed by connoisseurs and critics. Among the qualities that make Leonardo's works unique are the innovative techniques he used in the application of paint, his extensive knowledge of human and animal anatomy, botany and geology, but also his use of light, his interest in physiognomy and the way humans use the register of emotions and gestural expressions, his sense of composition and his subtle sense of color gradation. In particular, he mastered the technique of "sfumato" and the representation of light and shadow. All these qualities are present in his best known paintings, *the Mona Lisa*, the *Last Supper* and the *Virgin of the Rocks*.

Leonardo painted many portraits of women, but to date only one portrait of a man has been found, that of a musician. He is often attributed with the phrase that "the most praiseworthy figure is the one that best expresses the passions of the soul with its movement", which explains his thinking as a painter. However, he also drew caricatures of his contemporaries in the grotesque mode.

Leonardo is famous for his drawings and paintings in which he introduced an innovative concept of perspective. Da Vinci believed that the pictorial arts form a science. However, the use of the golden ratio in his work, often assumed, is not proven. His work on proportions, like *the Vitruvian Man, is limited to the* use of fractions of whole numbers.

"Painting is poetry that is seen rather than felt, and poetry is painting that is felt rather than seen." - Leonardo da Vinci

First works

Leonardo's earliest works begin with *The Baptism of Christ,* painted with Andrea del Verrocchio, to whom it is attributed, and his other pupils. Two other paintings in the studio seem to date from this period, both of which are "Annunciations"; one is small, fifty-nine centimeters wide and only fourteen centimeters high. It is a predella at the base of a larger composition, and in this case for a painting by Lorenzo di Credi from which it was separated. The other is a much larger work, two hundred and seventeen centimeters wide.

In these two annunciations, Leonardo depicted the Virgin Mary, seated or kneeling on the right of the image, and an angel in profile approaching her from the left. Much work has been done on the movements of the angel's clothing and wings. Although formerly attributed to Domenico Ghirlandaio, the work is now almost universally attributed to da Vinci.

In the smaller painting, Mary looks away and folds her hands in a gesture symbolizing submission to God's will. However, in the larger painting, Mary does not seem so docile; the young woman, interrupted in her reading by the unexpected messenger angel, places her finger on the sacred book to locate the page of her interrupted reading and raises her hand in a gesture of greeting or surprise. Her calmness seems to show that she accepts her role as Mother of God, not with resignation, but with confidence. In this painting, the young Leonardo presents the humanistic face of the Virgin Mary, recognizing the role of humanity in the incarnation of God. It is evident that this last painting was worked on by several people, since certain stylistic discontinuities can be appreciated, such as an "error" of perspective in Mary's right arm, the flowery meadow in the manner of embroidery or the angel's raptor wings. The style of the lectern of the painting could be a nod to the style of the tomb of Peter de Medici by Verrocchio in 1472.

Paintings from the 1480s

In the 1480s, Da Vinci received two very important commissions and began work on another work also of great compositional importance. Unfortunately, two of the three works were never completed and the third took so long to create that it was the subject of lengthy negotiations over its completion and payment. One of these paintings is *St. Jerome*. Liana Bortolon, in her book *The Life and Times of Leonardo* (1967), associates this painting with a difficult period in Leonardo's life. Signs of melancholy can be read in his diary: "I thought I was learning to live; I was only learning to die.

The composition of the painting is very unusual, although it is true that some parts were cut out. The painting represents the penitence of Jerome of Stridon in the desert. Penitent, Jerome occupies the center of the painting, with his body slightly diagonal. His kneeling posture adopts a trapezoidal shape, with one arm extended toward the outer edge of the painting and his gaze in the opposite direction. Jack Wasserman highlights the relationship between this painting and Leonardo's anatomical studies. In the foreground of the painting is his symbol, a large lion, whose body and tail form a double curve at the base of the painting. The other interesting feature is the surface appearance of the rocky landscape in which the figure is set.

The bold and innovative deployment of composition, with landscape elements and personal drama, is also evident in the great unfinished masterpiece *The Adoration of the Magi*, a commission from the monks of San Donato in Scopeto. It is a painting of very complex composition, and Leonardo made numerous preparatory drawings and studies, including a very detailed one for the linear perspective of a classical architectural ruin that serves as a backdrop to the scene. In 1482, however, Leonardo left for Milan, at the request of Lorenzo de' Medici, to win the graces of Ludovico Sforza. As a result, he abandoned painting.

The third important work of this period is *The Virgin of the Rocks*, commissioned in Milan for the Confraternity of the Immaculate Conception. The painting, realized with the help of the friars, was to fill a large altarpiece, already built. Leonardo chose to paint a passage from the infancy of Christ taken from the apocryphal Gospels, when the little John the Baptist, under the protection of an angel, meets the Holy Family on the road to Egypt. In this scene, painted by Leonardo da Vinci, John recognizes and adores Jesus as the Christ. The painting shows graceful figures kneeling in adoration before Christ in a rugged, rocky landscape. The painting is almost as complex as the one commissioned by the monks of San Donato, although it has only four figures-not fifty-and depicts a landscape rather than an architectural background. The painting was completed, but actually two versions of it were made: the one that remained in the confraternity's chapel and the one Leonardo took to France. But the brothers did not get their painting until the following century. A second version of this painting, with the addition of the halo and the staff of John the Baptist, was made some years later.

"Where the spirit does not work with the hand, there is no art. - Leonardo da Vinci

Paintings from the 1490s

Leonardo's most famous painting from the 1490s is *The Last Supper*. It is painted directly on a wall of the convent of Santa Maria delle Grazie in Milan. The painting depicts the last meal shared by Jesus and his disciples before his capture and death. It shows precisely the moment when Jesus declares: "one of you will betray me". Leonardo depicts the consternation that this statement provoked in Jesus' twelve disciples.

Matteo Bandello observed Leonardo at work and wrote in one of his accounts that some days he painted from dawn to dusk without even stopping to eat, and then did not paint for the next three or four days. According to Vasari, this provoked the incomprehension of the father superior, the prior, who expelled the painter until Leonardo asked for the intervention of the Duke of Milan, Ludovico Sforza. Vasari also describes how Da Vinci doubts his ability to paint the faces of Jesus and Judas correctly, and tells the duke that he may have used the monk as a model.

The finished fresco was hailed as a masterpiece of design and characterization, and was later admired by Peter Paul Rubens and Rembrandt. The work has been continually restored, with the paint detached from the plaster support. The painting deteriorated rapidly, to the point that, even before the centenary of its creation, it was described by a witness as "totally devastated". Leonardo, instead of using the tried and tested fresco technique, employed the "tempera technique", a painting process that uses egg yolk as a medium to bind the pigments, while the support is mainly "gesso", a type of chalk made from the mineral calcium carbonate, which produced a surface prone to mildew and flaking.

Despite these setbacks, the *Last Supper* has remained one of the most reproduced works of art. Fortunately, a large period canvas is on display at Tongerlo Abbey in Westerlo. It is one of the most faithful and oldest copies of the Italian masterpiece: the work of Leonardo's pupils, it seems that he himself painted the head of Jesus and that of the apostle John. The restorers came to Westerlo to get the exact colors for their work before going to Milan.

16th century paintings

Among the works created by Leonardo in the 16th century is a small portrait known as the *Mona Lisa* (1503-1506). The painting is known, in particular, for the elusive smile on the face of the woman, who experts agree is Lisa Gherardini. The quality of the painting may be due to the fact that the artist has subtly shaded the corners of the mouth and eyes, so that the exact nature of the smile cannot be determined. The quality of the shading, for which the work is renowned, has been called "sfumato". Giorgio Vasari wrote that "the smile is so pleasing that it seems divine rather than human; those who have seen it have been greatly surprised to find that it appears as vivid as the original." However, and for a long time, it has been generally accepted by experts that Vasari may never have known the painting other than by its fame, since he described it as having eyebrows. High-definition spectroscopic analysis has confirmed the hypothesis of

Daniel Arasse, who, in his book *Leonardo da Vinci* (1997), discussed the possibility that Leonardo may have painted the face with eyebrows, but that these were subsequently removed, in part because they were not fashionable in the mid-16th century. In fact, *the Mona Lisa* would have had eyebrows and eyelashes that were later removed.

Fact: A stroke left Leonardo's right hand paralyzed, truncating his pictorial career and leaving works such as "La Gioconda" unfinished.

Other characteristics of this work are the severity of the clothes, leaving the eyes and hands without other details, the dramatic background landscape, the color work and the nature of the painting technique, very soft, using oils, but spreading in a manner similar to tempera and blurring the surface, so that the brushstrokes seem inseparable. Vasari opined that the manner of painting would make even "the most confident of [painting] masters...despair and lose heart." The remarkable state of conservation and the fact that there are no visible signs of repairs or repainting are extremely rare for a painting of this period.

In *Saint Anne, Virgin and Child Jesus playing with a lamb*, the composition takes up the theme of figures in a landscape that Jack Wasserman, in his book *Leonardo da Vinci* (1975), describes as "striking in its beauty" and refers to the unfinished painting of *Saint Jerome* with the figure at an oblique angle with one of his arms. What makes *St. Anne, the Virgin and Child Jesus playing with a lamb* so rare is the presence of two sets in a different perspective, but superimposed. Mary is seated on the lap of her mother, St. Anne. She leans forward to hold the

46

infant Jesus, who is playing with a lamb, a sign of the imminence of his own sacrifice. This painting, copied several times, influenced Michelangelo, Raphael and Andrea del Sarto and, through them, Pontormo and Correggio. The style of the composition was adopted in particular by the Venetian painters Tintoretto and Paul Veronese.

Drawings and sketches

"The painter who draws simply by practice and by eye, without any reason, is like a mirror that copies everything that is put in front of it without being aware of its existence." - Leonardo da Vinci

Da Vinci was not a prolific painter, but he was a draftsman, filling his diaries with small sketches and detailed drawings to record everything that caught his attention. In addition to his sketches, there are numerous studies for his paintings, some of which can be considered preparatory for works such as *The Adoration of the Magi*, *The Virgin with the Rocks* and *The Last Supper*. His earliest dated drawing is a landscape, *Landscape of the Arno Valley* (1473), which shows in great detail the river, the mountains, the castle of Montelupo and the farms beyond.

Among his famous drawings are the *Vitruvian Man*, a study of the proportions of the human body, the *Head of a Young Girl* in Preparation for the Angel's Head in *The Virgin of the Rocks,* and Saint Anne, *the Virgin, the Infant Jesus and Saint John the Baptist as a Child,* which is a large (160 × 100 cm) black and white chalk on colored paper drawing of Saint Anne. Along with the Holy Family, this subject of St. Anne will dominate Leonardo's work from 1500 to 1517. This drawing employs the subtle technique of sfumato, in the manner of *the Mona Lisa*. It seems that Leonardo never made a painting from this drawing, but a painting quite similar is *St. Anne, the Virgin and Child Jesus playing with a lamb*.

Other drawings of interest are many studies generally called "caricatures" because, although exaggerated, they seem to be based on the observation of living models. Giorgio Vasari relates that if Leonardo saw a person with an interesting face, he would follow them around all day to observe them. There are many studies of handsome young men, often associated with Salai, with the rare, much admired and characteristic face known as the "Greek profile". These faces are often contrasted with those of a warrior. Salai is often depicted in costume and disguise. Leonardo is known to have designed sets for traditional processions. Other drawings, often meticulous, show studies of draperies. The Leon Bonnat Museum in Bayonne preserves a drawing by Leonardo da Vinci of Bernardo di Bandino Baronchelli (one of the assassins of Giuliano de' Medici during the Pazzi conspiracy), after he was hanged in one of the windows of the *Palace of the Captain of Justice* in Florence on December 29, 1479.

Leonardo as an observer, scientist and inventor

Leonardo da Vinci's childhood memories describe realistic and accurate observations of nature that he made at an early age and to which he attributed a certain dreamlike quality. For example, he carefully observed and described the flight of a kite, and came to imagine the animal landing in its cradle and opening its mouth with its tail. The discovery of a whale fossil in a cave near Florence awakens in him not only amazement at the strength and grandeur of the animal, but also fear of death or a possible deadly apocalypse. These events, which attest to a keen sense of observation, seem to stimulate his sense of scientific discovery, on the one hand, and his sense of imagination, on the other.

Diaries and notes

Renaissance humanism did not link science and art. However, Da Vinci's studies in the field of science and engineering are as impressive and innovative as his artistic work, recorded in notebooks comprising some thirteen thousand pages of writings and drawings, combining art and natural philosophy (the basis of modern science). These notes were made and updated daily throughout Leonardo's life and travels. He continually strove to make observations of the world around him, conscious and proud of being, as he defined himself, a "man without letters", self-taught and lucid about natural phenomena that often departed from what he had learned in school.

These diaries are, for the most part, written in Tuscan in a specular script better known as "mirror writing". The reason may be more practical, to be faster, than for reasons of encryption to escape the censorship of his time or to keep his working notes secret, as is often suggested (thesis of the 15th century mathematician Luca Pacioli, refuted because this script is easily read with the aid of a mirror, and Leonardo sprinkles his notes with abbreviations, and it is rather this feature that makes them difficult to read). As Leonardo wrote with his left hand, he must have found it easier to write from right to left. This is because the hand exerts less effort and this technique avoids leaving streaks or erasing wet ink when passing the hand over the pen. However, sometimes he writes from left to right, which shows that he has also mastered this technique.

His annotations and drawings, the earliest of which are dated 1475, show a wide variety of interests and concerns, but also some random lists of edibles or of his debtors.

There are compositions for paintings, studies of details and tapestries, studies of faces and emotions, animals, babies, dissections, botanical and geological studies, war machines, flying machines, and architectural works.

These notebooks - initially loose sheets of various sizes and types, donated by his friends after his death - have become part of important collections such as those on display at Windsor Castle, the Bibliothèque de l'Institut de France, the Biblioteca Nacional de España, the Biblioteca Ambrosiana in Milan, the Victoria and Albert Museum and the British Library in London. The British Library has placed a selection of its notes (*BL Arundel MS 263*) on the Internet on the pages of its website dealing with this chapter. The Codex Leicester is the only major scientific work by Da Vinci in the hands of a private owner (Bill Gates).

It appears that Leonardo's diaries were intended for publication, as many of the sheets have a shape and order that would facilitate editing. In many cases, a single subject, for example, the human heart or the fetus, is treated in detail in both words and pictures on a single sheet. This method of organization also minimizes the loss of data in the event that pages are mixed up or destroyed. It is unknown why these diaries were not published during Leonardo's lifetime, but some believe that society was not ready for them, especially the Church in relation to his anatomical work.

In 2019, a scientific study conducted by researchers at the Uffizi Museum in Florence proves that Leonardo da Vinci is ambidextrous based on the analysis of the drawing the *Paesaggio*.

Scientific studies

"Wisdom is the child of experience. - Leonardo da Vinci

Leonardo's approach to science is closely linked to observation: if "science is the captain, practice is the soldier". His science, his scientific research, refers exclusively to the parts he practiced as a technician. Leonardo da Vinci tried to understand a phenomenon by describing and illustrating it in great detail, without insisting on theoretical explanations. His studies on flight or the movement of water are probably the most remarkable in this respect. Because of his lack of initial instruction in Latin and mathematics, contemporary scholars have largely ignored the erudite Leonardo, although he taught himself Latin.

In the 1490s he studied mathematics with Luca Pacioli and made a series of drawings of regular solids in skeleton form to be recorded in his book *Divina Proportione* (1509). He was especially fascinated by the idea of the absolute and the universal. However, his mathematical culture was that of a practitioner: he had the limited aims of the abacists of his time, he penetrated with difficulty into the geometry of the Greeks, and his perspective was that of all the theorists of his time. However, beyond the simple geometrical aspect of the representation of perspective, he proposes in his Treatise on Painting a threefold definition of perspective:

1°: linear perspective (decrease in size of objects in proportion to their distance from the observer, geometric perspective ss),

2°: chromatic perspective (attenuation of colors in proportion to their distance from the observer),

3°: fading perspective (decrease in the precision of details in proportion to their distance from the observer).

In addition, Leonardo designed an instrument with an articulated system intended to construct a mechanical solution to Alhazen's problem, an essentially technical problem, and which demonstrates a knowledge of the laws of reflection.

Likewise, Leonardo's mechanics is that of his contemporaries, with its weaknesses, uncertainties and errors, and he does not seem to have made many discoveries in this field. His physics is rather confused and vague. He was certainly never an artilleryman and has no theory on ballistics. However, as some of his diagrams show, Leonardo da Vinci may have had the intuition, as could be seen in a water jet, that there was no straight part in the trajectory of an artillery projectile, contrary to what was commonly accepted at the time. However, he soon stopped on a path that Tartaglia and then Benedetti were to follow and which led to Galileo.

Although Alberti and Francesco di Giorgio Martini were concerned with the resistance of beams, they never sought mathematical formulations. Leonardo da Vinci became interested in the bending problem, no doubt with the help of experiments, and succeeded in defining laws, still imperfect, of the elastic line for beams of different sections, free or embedded, including Galileo's problem (*the balcony problem*). In doing so, he eliminated the modulus of elasticity and moment, to which Jordanus Nemorarius had alluded.

His chemistry was limited to the development of an alembic and some research on alchemy that he carried out in Rome.

Paul Valéry highlights the way in which Leonardo da Vinci discovered intuitively, through observation, "the first germ of the theory of luminous undulations", without being able, however, to validate it experimentally: "The air is full of infinite straight and radiating lines, intertwined and woven without one ever taking the path of another, and they represent for each object the true form of its reason (of its explanation).

Leonardo da Vinci also studied light and optics extensively; in hydrology, the only real law he formulated was that of the flow of rivers.

It appears from the contents of his notebooks that he planned to publish a series of treatises on a wide variety of subjects. On several occasions he mentions a draft *treatise on water*, but it seems that his thinking was so extensive that it seemed unfeasible. A treatise on anatomy is said to have been observed during a visit by the secretary of Cardinal Luis de Aragon in 1517.

His pupil, Francesco Melzi, tried to reconstruct the *Treatise on Painting* that Leonardo da Vinci had planned to write throughout his life. He compiled aspects of his work on anatomy, light and shade, drapery and landscapes. In 1651 a partial and incomplete edition of Francesco Melzi's work appeared, first in Italian and then in French. Charles Le Brun presented the French edition of the *Traité de la peinture to the* members of the Royal Academy of Painting and Sculpture as the book that would henceforth serve as their reference (despite Abraham Bosse's criticism and Félibien's skepticism). Leonardo da Vinci thus became "the forerunner of academic thought", according to Daniel Arasse.

Medicine and anatomy

Fact: Da Vinci dissected At first, the artist probably had to dissect largely in secret. Although dissection itself was not technically illegal, Leonardo found it difficult to obtain bodies. But as his reputation grew, it became easier to obtain cadavers, and by 1517 da Vinci is said to have performed more than 30 dissections.

Leonardo's initial training in the anatomy of the human body began during his apprenticeship with Andrea del Verrocchio, as his teacher insisted that all of his students learn anatomy. As an artist, he quickly became a master of topographical anatomy, drawing numerous studies of muscles, tendons, and other visible anatomical features. He laid the foundations of scientific anatomy, dissecting, among other things, the corpses of criminals with the strictest discretion, to avoid the Inquisition. Working conditions were particularly difficult due to the problems of hygiene and preservation of the bodies.

As a renowned artist, he was authorized to dissect human corpses at the hospital of Santa Maria Nuova in Florence and, later, at hospitals in Milan and Rome (from 1513 to

1516, he performed several autopsies at the Roman hospital *Santo Spirito in Sassia*). From 1487, he performed about twenty dissections to write a treatise on anatomy that was never published. From 1510 to 1511, he collaborated in his research with the physician Marcantonio della Torre.

Leonardo drew many human skeletons, bones, as well as muscles and tendons, the heart and vascular system, the action of the eye, sexual organs and other internal organs. These observations sometimes contain inaccuracies due to the ignorance of the time. For example, he never saw the circulation of the blood. However, he identified four chambers in the heart (Vesalius and Descartes saw only two), made one of the first scientific drawings of a fetus in the womb and the first scientific observation of the stiffness of arteries after a heart attack. As an artist, Leonardo closely observed the effects of age and human emotions on physiology, studying in particular the effects of anger. He also drew many models, some with severe facial deformities or visible signs of disease.

He also studied and drew the anatomy of many animals. He dissected cows, birds, monkeys, bears and frogs, comparing the anatomical structure of these animals with that of humans. He also studied horses.

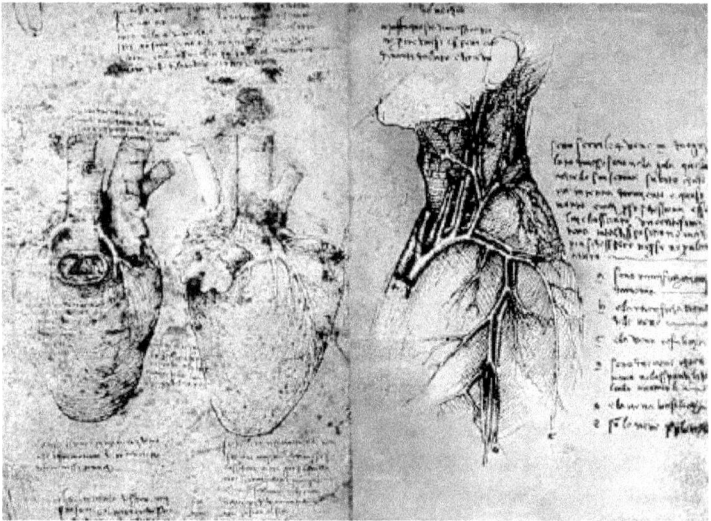

Engineering and invention

"How many biographies have been written that mention this scientific or technical activity only to show the breadth of a knowledge that claims to be universal [...] All this could only be done painfully, through constant research of what the ancients or immediate predecessors had written [...] And because of the ignorance of all this past that had made him, Leonardo was presented as a fertile inventor.

> - Bertrand Gille, in *Les ingénieurs de la Renaissance*

Leonardo da Vinci was part of the technical movement of the Renaissance and, as such, had immediate or more distant predecessors, such as Konrad Kyeser, Taccola, Roberto Valturio, Filippo Brunelleschi, Jacomo Fontana and Leon Battista Alberti, to whom he undoubtedly owed much.

Some had more powerful personalities, more complete minds and even more curious. This is the case of Francesco di Giorgio Martini, who was his superior during the construction of the Milan dome and from whom he surely borrowed a lot. Being undoubtedly less busy with his work than Martini due to a smaller order book, Leonardo da Vinci was more prolific, but above all capable of changing methods.

Legend has it that Leonardo was the forerunner of several modern machines, but many of them were invented by predecessors (such as the paddle wheel boat that existed under the Southern Song dynasty in the [5th] century, the helicopter, the tracked vehicle, the weaving machine for hydraulic saws, the submarine or the armored tank that Leonardo perfected after having extracted his ideas from the notebooks of Taccola and his master Giorgio, who in turn copied manuscripts of contemporary or medieval thinkers) and, beyond the amazement one feels at the author's prospective imagination, one quickly sees that the actual functioning of the machine must not have been his main concern. Like the monk Eilmer of Malmesbury in the 11th century, who forgot the tail on his flying machine, Leonardo's inventions run into numerous difficulties: the helicopter would fly like a spinning top, the diver would suffocate, the rowing boat would not move forward, the pyramid-shaped parachute would coil up on itself, and so on. Moreover, in these sketches, Leonardo never raises the problem of motive power.

In a *letter of application* to Ludovico Sforza, which is a real decalogue, he presents his professional profile, the best on the market, with skills and secrets that can really make the difference with all those who claim to be experts in war. He lists: bridges, scaffolding and ladders, tools to destroy walls and fortresses, siege machines, bombers and mortars, secret passages, tanks, weapons for naval battles, bomb-bearing ships, that is, all kinds of equipment that can be used both for city protection and siege.

"Human subtlety will never conceive of a more beautiful, simpler or more direct invention than that made by nature, because in her inventions nothing is lacking, and nothing is superfluous." - Leonardo da Vinci

When he fled to Venice in 1499, he found a job as an engineer and developed a system of movable barriers to protect the city from land attacks. He also planned to divert the flow of the Arno River to irrigate Tuscan fields, facilitate transportation and even hinder the maritime supply of Pisa, Florence's rival.

His notebooks contain a large number of "inventions" (his own inventions or improvements of machines and instruments) that are both practical and realistic, including hydraulic pumps, crank mechanisms such as the screw-cutting machine for wood, Hydraulic pumps are among them, crank mechanisms such as the screw-cutting machine, fins for mortar shells, a steam cannon· the submarine, various automatons, the tank, the automobile, floats for "walking on water," the solar energy concentrator, the calculator, the helmeted diving suit, the double helmet, and the ball bearing. The authorship of the bicycle is highly controversial.

However, a close examination of these writings indicates that many of these techniques were borrowed from a few immediate predecessors (the hydraulic turbine by Francesco di Giorgio Martini, the articulated chain for the transmission of movements by Taccola, etc.), or the heritage of an even older tradition (the hydraulic hammer is known in the 13th century, siphons and aqueducts can be seen in Frontino, and the automata for entertainment described by Greek mechanics, etc.). But Leonardo was also an innovator; he was certainly one of the first engineers of the time to be interested in the mechanical working of metal, and in particular of gold, which was more malleable. Along with the flying machine, the few textile machines, in which the regularity of the movements used allowed him to apply his sense of observation, marked his originality. The power loom, the carding machine and the shearing machine made Leonardo the first to mechanize industrial production. The mirror polishing machine, which involved solving a series of problems to obtain regular, flat or concave surfaces, was devised during his stay in Rome, when he was studying the manufacture of images. Paradoxically, Leonardo took little interest in inventions that today we consider very important, such as the printing press, although he is one of the first to give us a representation of a printing press.

Although war is a necessity, it is a pazzia bestialissima ("savage madness"). For this reason, he studies weapons while staying away from their use.

In 1502, Leonardo designed a two hundred and forty meter bridge as part of a civil engineering project for the Ottoman Sultan Bayezid II of Istanbul. The bridge was intended to cross the mouth of the Bosphorus, known as the Golden Horn. Beyazid did not carry out the project, as he felt that construction would be impossible. However, in 2019 the Massachusetts Institute of Technology demonstrated that the bridge would have been quite feasible. In 2001, a small bridge based on these plans was built in Norway. On May 17, 2006, the Turkish government decided to build the Leonardo Bridge for the Golden Horn.

For most of his life, Leonardo was, like Icarus, fascinated by flight. He carried out numerous studies on this phenomenon, drawing inspiration from birds and from the flight plans of various devices, such as the first stages of the helicopter known as the "aerial screw", the parachute and a kind of hang glider made of bamboo. Most of these were unfeasible, but the hang glider was built and, with the addition of a tail unit for stability, flew successfully. However, it seems likely that he thought bat-like systems had the greatest potential. He also invented the aerodynamic wind tunnel for his work.

The Clos Lucé Museum in Amboise, the *Il Castello* Museum in the castle of the Counts Guidi da Vinci and the Leonardo da Vinci Museum of Science and Technology contain numerous models, life-size objects based on the study of his notebooks and explanations of his work.

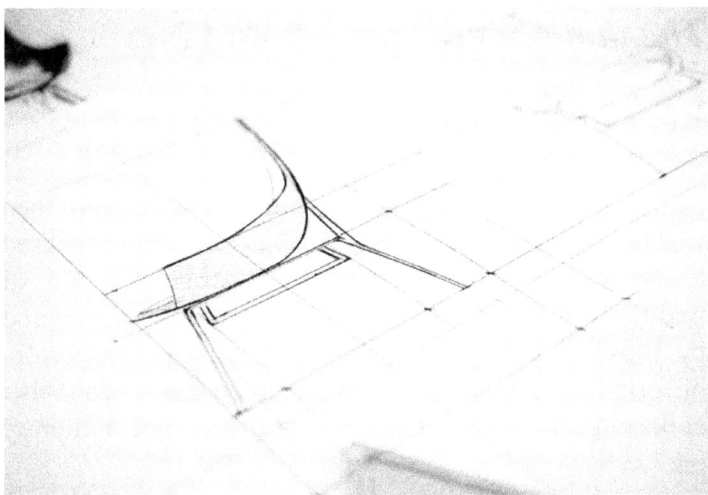

Da Vinci also studied architecture. Influenced by the work of Filippo Brunelleschi, he planned to erect the Baptistery of St. John in Florence or create a lantern tower for the Milan cathedral. He often used the octagonal shape for religious buildings and the circle for military buildings. In the wake of the plague that ravaged Milan between 1484 and 1485, he designed a theoretically perfect city, with optimal circulation routes and quality living conditions; his vision was not marked by social distinctions, but was functional, like the organs of a human body. He also works in gardens. However, much of his architectural work will be lost.

The thought of Leonardo da Vinci

Leonardo da Vinci's method

Leonardo da Vinci had a need to rationalize that until then was unknown to technicians. With him, technique ceased to be a thing of craftsmen, of ignoramuses and of traditions more or less valid and more or less understood by those in charge of applying them. George Sarton, historian of science, indicates that Leonardo da Vinci collected an "oral and manual tradition, not a literary one".

It is mainly through failures, mistakes and catastrophes that he tries to define the truth: cracks in walls, destructive undermining of banks, poor mixing of metals are opportunities to learn about good practices.

Gradually, he developed a kind of technical doctrine, born of observations soon followed by experiments sometimes performed on small models. Harald Höffding presents his thought as a mixture of empiricism and naturalism. Indeed, if for Leonardo da Vinci "*wisdom is the daughter of experience*", the latter allows him to constantly verify his intuitions and theories, because "experience is never wrong; it is his judgments that are wrong in promising effects that are not caused by his experiments".

Leonardo's method undoubtedly consisted in the search for numerical data and his interest in measuring instruments attests to this. These data were relatively easy to obtain in the case of bending beams, for example, but much more complicated in the case of arches or masonry.

The formulation of the results could only be simple, i.e., expressed mostly by ratios. This frantic pursuit of precision became Leonardo's motto, Hostinato rigore ('stubborn rigor'). However, this is the first time that these methods have been applied in the trades, where unreasonable means of evaluation have long been the norm.

In this way, Leonardo became capable of posing problems in general terms. What he sought above all was general knowledge that could be applied in all cases and that would provide the means to act on the material world. However, his "technical science" remains fragmentary. It focuses on a number of specific problems, treated in a very limited way, but still lacks the overall coherence that his successors would soon find.

For him, this search in all areas of science and art is normal, because everything is related. His curiosity and perpetual activity are the means to keep his mind alive, for "iron rusts if it is not used, stagnant water loses its purity and freezes in the cold. In the same way, inaction saps the vigor of the mind". Leonardo da Vinci saw painting, for example, as the visual expression of a whole; art, philosophy and science were, in his view, inseparable and could partly explain his polymathic approach and "He who blames painting loves neither philosophy nor nature." By proposing a "synthesis through beauty", Leonardo da Vinci alone illustrates what the great innovation of the Renaissance consisted of.

However, this attempt at a great synthesis - art and science - was a failure and marked the "growing and definitive" separation of the fields of art and science, and thus the beginning of the modern era.

Morals and ethics

"You can have no greater or lesser mastery than that over yourself." - Leonardo da Vinci

Leonardo da Vinci believes that man must be actively committed to fighting evil and doing good, since "he who neglects to punish evil contributes to provoking it." He also indicates that he has no illusions about the nature of man and the use he can make of his inventions, as he does in a preamble to a presentation of the submarine:

"I do not describe my method of staying under water nor how long I can remain there without eating. And I do not publish or divulge them, because of the evil nature of men, who would use them to murder at the bottom of the sea by destroying the ships by sinking them and the men they carry."

Leonardo da Vinci also places moral rewards far above material ones:

"It is not riches, which can be lost. Virtue is our true good and the true reward of its possessor. It cannot be lost, it cannot forsake us, except when life flees."

Vegetarianism

Leonardo da Vinci, known in his lifetime for buying caged birds to set them free, was also famous for being a vegetarian because he refused to harm animals (in the manner of the "*guzzarati*" or Hindus), which may place him in line with the philosophy of Pythagoras or Empedocles of Agrigento (who also inspired Giordano Bruno). Leonardo da Vinci wrote in this regard:

"Man, if you really are, as you describe, the king of the animals,-I would have said rather the king of the brutes, the greatest of all! - why do you take your subjects and children to satisfy your palace, for reasons that make you a grave for all animals? [...] Does not nature produce simple food in abundance? And if you cannot satisfy yourselves with such simple foods, why do you not prepare your meals by mixing these [plant-based] foods in a sophisticated way?

- Quaderni d'Anatomia II 14 r.

The posterity of Leonardo da Vinci

Leonardo da Vinci perfectly embodies the spirit of the Renaissance, the era of the "Great Discoveries". A universal genius, curious about everything, sometimes considered as a character between Faust and Plato, he dedicated his life to the pursuit of knowledge. He imagined many devices and machines, including the first "flying machine", which remained at the drawing stage. More than as a scientist in the strict sense of the word, Leonardo da Vinci impressed his contemporaries and later generations by his methodical approach to knowledge, learning, observation and analysis. His approach to all the activities he tackled, both in art and technique - the two were indistinguishable in his mind - especially in watchmaking, was based on a prior accumulation of detailed observations, of knowledge scattered here and there, tending to surpass what already existed, with perfection as the goal. Many of Leonardo's sketches, notes and treatises are not, strictly speaking, original discoveries, but the result of research carried out in an encyclopedic spirit, before his time. "Leonardo da Vinci does not classify well and it is in this sense that he has seemed exceptional.

During his lifetime, Leonardo was already so famous that King Francis I took him to France as a trophy, and claimed to have accompanied him in his old age and held him in his arms when he died. *The death of Leonardo da Vinci,* as depicted by Domenico Ingres, is however an apparently very romantic vision. In reality, Francis I was probably in Saint-Germain-en-Laye at the time of his death, as he signed a royal edict there the day after Leonardo's death, on May 3.

Interest in da Vinci has never waned since. Giorgio Vasari, in *Le Vite,* 1568 edition, introduces his chapter on Leonardo da Vinci with the following words:

"In the normal course of events, many men and women are born with remarkable talents; but sometimes, in a way that transcends nature, a person is wonderfully endowed by heaven with beauty, grace and talent in such abundance that he leaves other men far behind. All his actions seem inspired and, in fact, everything he does clearly comes from God and not from human ability. Everyone recognizes that this was true of Leonardo da Vinci, an artist of astonishing physical beauty, who showed infinite grace in everything he did and who cultivated his genius so brilliantly that every problem he studied he solved with ease."

Giorgio Vasari thus laid the foundations of the myth of Leonardo da Vinci: a perfect painter, courtly and handsome, a gloomy genius fascinated by ugliness, but incapable of completing his work. Vasari's anecdotes have been repeated and reworked in biographies of Leonardo da Vinci up to the present day.

The continued admiration of painters, critics and historians for Leonardo is reflected in many other written tributes. Baldassare Castiglione, author of the *Book of the Courtier*, wrote in 1528: "Another of the greatest painters in the world, who looks down on his art, in which he has no peer," while the biographer "Anonimo" Gaddiano wrote around 1540: "He was so exceptional and universal that he may be said to have been born of a miracle of nature."

Leonardo *da Vinci's* writings were not published until a century after his death; the bilingual French-Italian edition of his *Treatise on Painting (Trattato della pittura di Leonardo da Vinci)* was published in Paris in 1651. His paintings were not studied at the time; they were only rediscovered, as were his *Notebooks* (the first notebook studied corresponds to unpublished extracts from the manuscripts of the Codex Atlanticus that the Italian physicist Giovanni Battista Venturi deciphered in 1797 in Paris), in the 18th and especially the 19th centuries, which saw in him a prophet of modernity.

The 19th century introduced a certain admiration for Leonardo's genius, with Johann Heinrich Füssli writing in 1801: "Such was the dawn of modern art, when Leonardo da Vinci appeared with a splendor that surpassed the usual excellence: composed of all the elements that constitute the very essence of genius", which is echoed by A. E. Rio, who wrote in 1861: "He was above all other artists thanks to the strength and nobility of his talents". The variety of Leonardo's field of application, conveyed by his notebooks, is well known, as are his paintings. Hippolyte Taine wrote in 1866: "There is probably no example in the world of a genius so universal, so capable of self-realization, so full of longing for the infinite, so naturally refined, so far ahead of his own and later centuries". The celebrated art historian Bernard Berenson wrote in 1896: "Leonardo is an artist of whom it can be said with perfect literalness: everything he has touched has been transformed into a thing of eternal beauty. Whether it be the cross-section of a skull, the structure of a grass or a study of muscles, with his sense of line and of light and shade, he has transformed it forever into values that communicate life. Charles Baudelaire even quotes him in *Les Fleurs du mal* (1857).

Interest in the genius Leonardo has not ceased, and experts study and translate his writings, analyze his paintings with scientific techniques, discuss the works attributed to him, and search for works recorded but never discovered. Art critic Liana Bortolon (it) writes in her book *The Life and Times of Leonardo* (1967): "Because of the multiplicity of interests that impelled him to pursue all fields of knowledge, [...] Leonardo can rightly be considered the universal genius par excellence and with all the harmony inherent in that term. Man is as uncomfortable with genius today as he was in the 16th century. Five centuries have passed and we still look at Leonardo with great awe. Crowds still line up to see his most famous works of art: for example, the Louvre Museum owes much of its fame to the *Mona Lisa*.

70

"Good writing comes from good talent. - Leonardo da Vinci

With the best-selling *Da Vinci Code,* a novel that combines historical facts and biblical resources, Dan Brown gave new impetus to the interest in da Vinci in 2003. The novel was adapted into a film by Ron Howard.

According to an article in Le *Monde*, the Tata Nano's gearbox was based on a Leonardo da Vinci model: it was simply a truncated cone-shaped lantern that was probably difficult to maneuver to keep in contact with the gear in which it engaged.

In 2007, a couple of Italian researchers hypothesized the presence of a hidden musical score inside the *Last Supper*. The arrangement of the hands of the figures and the bread on the table would give a little melody.

On April 26, 2008, a parachute jump was performed with a parachute designed according to Leonardo da Vinci's sketches and texts dating back to 1485. Swiss Olivier Vietti-Teppa jumped from a hovering helicopter 650 meters above the Payerne military airport with a replica of the parachute made of modern materials: he measured a fall speed of 3.9 m/s and was able to land normally. In 2000, the British Adrian Nicholas also jumped with a replica of the parachute, but being more faithful to the original, it weighed 80 kg and it was risky to land with it. The man abandoned the replica in flight to make a landing with a real parachute.

On December 18, 2008, during a restoration, staff members of the Louvre Museum in Paris discovered three

71

drawings depicting a horse's head, a skull and a child on the back of *Saint Anne, the Virgin and Child Jesus playing with a lamb*, probably by Leonardo da Vinci.

In France, in 2015, 94 schools were named after him, a rare occurrence for a foreign personality.

On November 15, 2017, his painting *Salvator Mundi,* recognized as authentic in 2005, sold in New York at Christie's for $450.3 million, making it the most expensive painting in the world and in history.

On the occasion of the 500th anniversary of his death in 2019, the Louvre Museum in Paris is dedicating an eventful exhibition to him with a large number of masterpieces attributed to Leonardo da Vinci.

CPSIA information can be obtained
at www.ICGtesting.com
Printed in the USA
BVHW032349050822
643962BV00011B/799